THE
CORONER'S
WIFE

The Coroner's Wife

Dryad Press (Pty) Ltd
Postnet Suite 281, Private Bag X16, Constantia, 7848, Cape Town
www.dryadpress.co.za

Cover design: Stephen Symons
Cover artwork: John Buckland Wright (Dover Publications, INC., New York)
Editor: Michèle Betty
Copy editor: Helena Janicsh
Proofreader: Juanita Louw
Typography: Stephen Symons
Set in 9.5/14pt Palatino Linotype regular
Printed and bound by Digital Action (Pty) Ltd
Photograph of Joan Hambidge on inside cover flap: Brenda Veldtman

First published in Cape Town, South Africa by Dryad Press 2018

ISBN: 978-0-6399141-2-1

Joan Hambidge is the recipient of the following literary awards:
The Eugène Marais Prize (1987) for *Bitterlemoene*
The Litera-prys (2001) for her poem on Eugène Marais in *Lykdigte*
The ATKV poetry prize (2012) for her collection *Visums by verstek*

THE
CORONER'S
WIFE

POEMS IN TRANSLATION

JOAN HAMBIDGE

With translations By Charl JF Cilliers,
Johann de Lange, Jo Nel and
Douglas Reid Skinner

People! Read Poetry

Dryad Press
Cape Town

for Johann de Lange

Here, take this sand that I pour
From one palm to another

– Osip Mandelstam

That was their business. As far as he was concerned.
Suffering was life's penalty; wisdom armed one
Against madness; speech was temporary; poetry was truth.

– Robert Pinsky, 'Essay on Psychiatrists'

CONTENTS

Section I

Travelogues

He's forgotten utterly where he is.
He's forgotten Paddington, forgotten
Timetables, forgotten the long rocking
Cradle of a journey into the golden West...

– Ted Hughes

Tokyo, a Meditation

– translation by Charl JF Cilliers

Does silence have a structure? you ask in a late-night email
to me, in another time zone, already light,
while I struggle with wifi in a hotel room at the Shiba Park.
My reply keeps getting stuck, skittish, floundering
like a fish about to lose its *ki*.
Just behind the hotel, there is a funeral parlour,
a karaoke bar and a park for indolent walks.
This email's like a smouldering fire, I reply.
There is still no online connection.
Yesterday at the temple, I washed my hands, left a coin.
Like me, the gods here are silent in all the conflicting languages.
In an unsent email, an unobtrusive scorching silence.

Tokyo, a Meditation II
– translation by Charl JF Cilliers

A Nokia with a belly full of sms-es,
a Dell Vostro with files full of recollections
and photos taken with a digital camera,
two inboxes swelling by the day.
I detach myself from these messages,
reminders, registrations. *You've got mail!*
the inbox rants in the Shiba Park Hotel.
Earlier, such a room shared, or longing
for another, the one who is always absent or leaving.
Now the hotel room a solace, more than a bed
in a city without street numbers, flickering neon.
The city a halfway house, a *bardo*.
The Orient, unknown, finger pointing to the West.
And you? You are already in San Francisco, reading Borges,
with a glass of Francis Coppola's Merlot, waiting
for a message from me, almost in the Pickwick Hotel.
I will tell you everything about Tokyo and how a poem
has me trapped in a Borges labyrinth until you read it.

Los Angeles, a Meditation

– translation by Charl JF Cilliers

Like a tracker moving through dense bush foraging
for the faintest signs, I walk in this city past
a hotel where I had lingered, a youngster in a leather jacket.
Then, Hollywood and all its tinsel was captivating.
I worshipped James Dean and Marilyn Monroe.
Saw the models for *Jaws* and countless other thrillers.
Framing the sign according to Culler, and I, the word sleuth,
wandering past the signatures in cement.
Dean and Monroe are gone now, yet they live on;
just like the person I was: self-focused, fearless
and, yes, fleeing so many painful incidents and losses:
the bloody memories dog my footsteps, even now.
The token as target? Everything here for the semiotic.
My hotel, the Wilshire Grand, will be demolished later this year.
Reader, let her off lightly; she was in essence defenceless.

New York, a Meditation

– translation by Charl JF Cilliers

During a sleepless night in the city that never sleeps,
a flickering billboard depicts a small man walking.
Tonight I remember the many people with grime on their faces
on the Brooklyn Bridge, milling away from those two buildings.
First the actual event, then the many representations.
Photographed from various angles, reproduced and multiplied.
A memorial flame burns; photos on walls,
flowers, crosses, interviews with next of kin keep
the memory alive: pain is a somnambulist
for which there is no cure, not then, not now.
A policeman's cap, one pair of shoes and a child's toy
exhibited in a museum. Only the shoes make sense
as a symbol: to keep on walking, moving, wordlessly fleeing
from this senseless act with no protection
on that day, called 9/11, when this city
was declared for evermore an incurable insomniac.

Istanbul, a Meditation

– translation by Charl JF Cilliers

In a turbid dream,
I tear out the inside page of a book,
where the library's date stamp is found.
The book is about them, the ones who've died,
the ones who are leaving, who often
appear in dreams, or who in foreign cities,
look exactly like local inhabitants,
but speak a foreign language; those who look up
amazed and never return a greeting, or who
lie outstretched in a glass case in a museum,
staring fixedly through unseeing eyes. Their lives
were on loan. Never belonged to them.
Their lives were merely a story; and the Author's name
in the colophon, a pseudonym.
That Name is the one I am still searching for.
Tonight I read from a borrowed book
about the lives of my friends, my father
and everyone who has crossed my path.
About a life taken from the library of the Dead.

Too Stony for Trees

– translation by Charl JF Cilliers

Where the ruins of Machu Picchu lie,
at Gallipoli and Cappadocia,
and en route to the road Paul travelled,
as in Hiroshima and Nagasaki,
I always pick up stones.
A small round stone to quench my thirst.
Don't larger stones of darker blue reveal
a bloody struggle or nuclear war?
Stones are mementos; or rather, bear witness.
They're silent interpreters of history,
are shaped by time and the shocks of the world:
stones of war, shingles, landmarks
on the eventual road to Damascus.

Tokyo

– translation by Charl JF Cilliers

One morning I stood in the fish market
watching the tuna, *nori* and *aji* on display.
A practised fisherman, in yellow rubber boots,
gutted a fish with a single stroke, its mouth agape.
From the stomach, entrails spewed
amidst a bloody stench. Also memories
from a deep-sea existence completely cut off
from earthquakes and bombs raining down.
He does not know Mt Fuji, and a light snowfall
(like soft down over the ocean) remains an oddity.
Edu's air pollution has never troubled him.
Once, he was a fish darting through water.
Now he is placed on ice for *sashimi*.
Before long he will end up in the ocean again,
piecemeal – altogether a non-fish –
travelling from hand to mouth: to human waste.

Kervansaray

– translation by Charl JF Cilliers

A small matchbox,
kervansaray international holiday courts,
packed with memories and impressions.
Mementos collected in so many cities:
from Havana, soap, its fragrance lost; a fold-up toothbrush
from Acapulco's Zen Hotel; a tube of toothpaste from Kyoto.
I play *Alice In Wonderland:* grow larger and smaller
before all the travel doors of my memory.
There was a time when I drowned in my tears: a tolling bell
of parting, rejection, the end of a relationship,
impelled the journey. The ginger cat's smile lingers.
One late-summer afternoon I drove into Edinburgh,
stood amazed at the pink tinge of a city
ablaze with the colours of sunset.
Now it is an inward journey in this knowledge: all
my impressions are imaged in this small matchbox.

Dublin
Baile Átha Cliath
– translation by Charl JF Cilliers

Obedientia Civium Urbis Felicitas

Dubhlinn
or black pool
takes me back to my youth
in a rural library, during
a winter vacation, where I, between
Scylla and Charybdis, explored every
reference in *Ulysses*. All eighteen episodes,
with careful attention, via Stuart Gilbert
on a literary sleuthing quest. Leopold Bloom and Molly's
sex scene and Stephen Dedalus as Telemachus.
Life, a nightmare from which I try to wake.
No. 7 Eccles Street smells of fried pig's kidneys.
Where is Paddy Dignam's grave in Glasnevin?
In Burton's Restaurant, an imagined glass of wine is waiting.
I am the cyclops, wandering, stumbling,
me again as Lydia Douce and Mina Kennedy exit,
Says I, says I, says I. In Ithaca,
a soothsayer prophesies a life-on-the-run.
Poetry springs forth from the banal, a mere composition
of lists: procrastination is the thief of time…
A latter-day Odysseus, not Penelope?
I hitchhike through the streets of Dublin
in Joyce's footsteps, and *my* stream of consciousness
takes me back to *that* space:
young chronicler of words oblivious of how
a poem unlocks an Old Mutual diary
full of lost, forgotten scribbles.

Santiago de Chile
– translation by Charl JF Cilliers

O beloved, tormented city:
I discern your distress,
your Costanero Norte cut off,
Santiaguinos trapped in
your dark underground and *Estacion*.
In my mind I walk across
the Alameda and wonder if Sanhattan
is still standing. Is the snow on the Andes melting?
Does the Cordillera de la Costa
know of your setback? Is Mapocho flourishing?
Is the Tupungato volcano
dormantly spluttering?
O beloved, tormented city:
La Chascona, that monument,
is hopefully unscathed?
Beyond the country's walls,
beside the snow's crystal lattice,
behind the river's green leafiness,
under the nitrate and thorns,
I came upon drops of blood,
and every drop burned
like fire. The words of the poet
of La Chascona remain
alive in me all the way to Machu Picchu
and the morning glow of the Urubamba's
soulful sounds of longing.

Acapulco

– translation by Charl JF Cilliers

From Mexico City with its violence and foul air,
I flee to your mythical, dream-conjured space.
In your scorching heat, I lie low in a retro hotel,
and my childhood days unwind like a home movie.
I smell the sweat and chlorine of the swimming pool,
a man laughs boisterously, a woman breaks a glass
and the ashtray with an Aztec symbol is full.
The film breaks, but no one switches on the light.
In the dark, the children are deliberating.
In the room next door, a woman is climbing the pyramid
of ecstasy, while the man apparently holds
back for a final swerve over the *corniche*
in Acapulco, which (unlike the Peter Stuyvesant
advert) takes me back to where I don't want to be.

Bangkok
Krung Thep Mahanakhon
– translation by Charl JF Cilliers

City of Angels,
Big City,
Eternal City of Jewels,
impenetrable city,
how does one evoke you in my language,
not in Pali or Sanskrit?
In your words you are called
Krung Thep Mahanakhon Amon Rattanakosin Mahinthara
Yuthaya Mahadilok Phop Noppharat Ratchathani Burirom
Udomratchaniwet Mahasathan Amon Phiman Awatan
Sathit Sakkathattiya Witsanukam Prasit,
city with the longest name on earth,
according to Lonely Planet.
My poetry needs something more passionate, more urgent:
for me, you are the Venice of the East
with your rivers and canals properly protected
against inundations and floods and other calamities.
Who watches over you?
In my imagination, I see
children sailing on *khlongs*
during jubilant festivals
and on Queen Sirikit's birthday,
so it is said, there are cheerful decorations and lights
in her honour. Angelic, bounteous, I am told,
like feverish rice-picking
in a Brahmin festive season,
and to perhaps gain some fleeting
understanding of you?
Without ceremony
or long-windedness,

your excess articulated in your name.
I do not understand you:
could never trim
you down: even though I was there.

Rome

– translation by Johann de Lange

Although I lost my religion a long time
before my virginity – traumatic for sure – in
imitation of others – I counterfeited – in Rome,
the original most original city of the arts, I understood
why artists create sculptures,
passionately render a painting
suspended from ceilings for the glory of art.
I must confess: I even cried with emotion

before Michelangelo's *Pietà*,

because it was so much more than just a mother
melancholically uncomprehending the death
of her firstborn – look at the fingers
stretching beyond the child's cold, bent knee,
the head pulled back, the loin cloth
already unravelling – how long before the body
decomposes? The muscles retreat, already slack.

Even the holes in hand and foot
reproduced in such unbelievably fine
detail (He was pierced through).

For me, death here seems colder than marble.

Las Vegas, Nevada

– translation by Charl JF Cilliers

Here, gambling dens take their appointed
place beside churches, and in a Greyhound,
leather-jacketed and rucksacked, she enters the City of Sin.
With an *achy-breaky heart*, the desert becomes
the perfect backdrop for a downtown motel
where travellers and whores briefly linger.
Fear and Loathing in Las Vegas. Behind her lies
the City of Angels and ahead of her Miami. Now,
in the moment, she confronts the Mohave Desert,
replicated in restaurants throughout the world,
complete with cactus and rock. For her it's hell,
this flickering city with its prayer beads and $ signs.
La$ Vegas. Lush Vegas. *Leaving Las Vegas.*
In the Liberace Museum, brother George sells
signatures on behalf of the virtuoso performer.
A bookshop displays Barthes's *Mythologies.*
Together, she and the semiologist interpret the xeriscapes,
simulations, illustrations, flickering lights: dollar a fuck.
She leaves Vegas, en route to Dallas, in search
of The American Dream, the greening of America:
of something that shimmers like a mirage in the desert.

Dallas, Texas

– translation by Charl JF Cilliers

On the trail of JFK, there where Zapruder
shot the cavalcade, governor John Connally in front,
Jacqueline in back, in Dealey Plaza: November 22, 1963.
Lee Harvey Oswald (*I'm the patsy*) murdered by Jack Ruby.
Mr President, you can't say Dallas doesn't love you,
the governor's wife said, and between frames 155 and 169,
everyone turned left and then right except the President.
The shot between frames 210 and 225 does not reveal blood
or tiny shards of bone: another shot hits from behind.
A certain James Tague, a casual observer, exactly 162m away,
was struck by a ricochet, and in the Parklands Hospital
John F Kennedy was declared dead by Dr George Burkley.
A Roman Catholic priest conducted the last sacraments.
In the autopsy report, every wound was accurately recorded.
In Air Force One, Lyndon B Johnson was sworn in.
The 1961 Lincoln Continental limousine stands in the Henry Ford
in Dearborn, Michigan, with the stained pink dress neatly stored.
Bullets, the gun, even the hospital trolley and autopsy report
on exhibit for the tourist, with an X marking the spot
of the first shot. The hideout of the alleged hitman
authentically reconstructed here in Dallas, Texas.
Believe what I say. All that and even more. On the trail of JFK.

Photo: Man Falling

– translation by Johann de Lange

Above heaven and earth,
this man
hangs vertically, crucified by
a photographer:

first an anonymous exclamation mark
on the day of reckoning
fleeing
fire and brimstone
away
far away
to existence outside of time
(and pain).

Many question marks follow:
who was this man?

The mystery solved:
we learn he was one Norberto Hernandez
from Puerto Rico. This was his last
working day as baker
and cup-bearer of life.

But in truth, he was an angel
who during this Armageddon
conquered the unbearable brittleness
of living.

Ground Zero

– translation by Johann de Lange

These travellers had no need to
pack a bag,
extend a visa,
or walk through customs.
There is no jet lag
or frustration with a foreign language,
exchange rates or insomnia.

Because the flight has landed
before their uncalled-for departure.

Section II

Love and Family

Love is a shadow.
How you lie and cry after it
Listen: these are its hooves: it has gone off, like a horse.

– Sylvia Plath

Aubade

– translation by Douglas Reid Skinner

The relentless timekeeping of the psyche,
those beacons of the mind:
small victories, above all the losses
lingering in the memory.

In dreams, the journal of the soul,
I briefly shuffle back in time,
back to you on another continent,
celebrating your birthday without me.

I pick up two stones for you, a birthday gift,
at Pablo Neruda's Isla Negra home.
The morning song of a small thrush,
overjoyed at another day's dawn.

In this *Plano de Ubicación*
we celebrate together in words,
another year of subtracting, adding and timekeeping.
The dawn has a poem in its mouth.

Aubade II

– translation by Douglas Reid Skinner

For what
are we waiting,
you and I?
Because the birds
on my top balcony
take me back
to the *probatio pennae*
of the medieval monk:
omnes uolucres nidos inceptos
nisi ego et tu quid expectamus nu(nc).
These pigeons argue over West Flemish:
hebban olla vogala nestas hagunnan
hinase hic enda thu wat unbidan we nu,
clichéd and rutting
like a couple of Hugh
Hefner-conscripted porn stars.
I shoo them on this Sunday morning,
knowing only shit will be left behind.
My missing you during these days
of arson, strikes and so much more,
makes me think: *#Aubademustfall.*

Name

– translation by Douglas Reid Skinner

I could never ever say your name,
just as you never ever wished
to name our secret love.
Your lengthy double-barrelled name
has lingered far too long in my mind
like a black forget-me-not.
Now, at last, I've said your name;
in a small ritual, I purify myself,
chancing to find an amulet this morning:
a healing, protective dizain.

Dream

– translation by Charl JF Cilliers

In the departure lounge of an airport,
you asked me to take your cases
along on that journey.
Without words, you whisper to me
through the cold glass where lovers
take their leave, and turn with one last backward glance
at someone moving through customs.
You taught me everything about how-to-travel-alone,
about poems heavily weighed down by stamps,
visas to unknown regions of the heart.
In that departure lounge of my dream,
I hunt, bewildered, for my own luggage,
find my suitcase in the arrivals hall,
filled to bursting with poems and dreams
and myths and small tablets and fears.
A dream is an apostrophe, a palindrome,
it leaves something out and adds something in.
It is a pointing finger, a colon,
a reflection – perhaps an arrivals hall
where the loved one, the all-comprehending reader,
meets you with a silent profusion of words?

State of Emergency
– translation by Jo Nel

In terms of the Fear of Further Involvement Act,
the Minister of Emotions imposed, this very morning,
a state of emergency on you my beloved, besieged city,
with emergency regulations and curfews
(I may no longer love you at sunset);
a draft paper
(no further meaningful communication);
riotous, passionate meetings between us
are prohibited;
breakfasts together, telephone calls,
meander in the labyrinth of reminiscences.

But I, the eternal revolutionary,
distribute leaflets in the dark, inciting a *coup d'état*.
I combat these infuriating laws,
wave banners furiously in the town square,
incite passers-by, unaware of the effect
this has on me (and hopefully on you).
Now, I will go underground in devastating anguish,
but I, the eternal revolutionary,
will fight on against man-made laws
and proclamations, which you, my besieged one,
so recklessly silent, so silently reckless,
accept and endure.

Verbal Commitment
– originally written in English by Joan Hambidge

There is a climate for commitment,
changes like rain on a winter morning:
sunlight to misty, dark clouds.
But we both know the weather forecast
of *love* (over-defined, romanticised
and cheapened) called climate-for-commitment:
lazy afternoons in discreet hideaways;
tea-for-two in chic restaurants;
dinners by candlelight
amidst other commitments.

There is a climate for commitment
sans unpredicted predictabilities:
meeting-passion-boredom-farewell...
I'd rather define you in a sealed envelope,
in a landscape of caring;
in a cat's cradle of intellectual *jouissance;*
in a body of writing –
so read this poem,
and rewrite me.

Meditation, Family

– translation by Charl JF Cilliers

I place gifts under the Christmas tree.
All at once I recall one Christmas Eve:
a hotel in Switzerland and a television programme
where the presenter was doling out good wishes.
A line stubbornly engaged, what would I do
if you were to answer? Or if the other party
picked up the phone? Peals of laughter from Joan Rivers
in *The Fashion Police*; my mom plays Solitaire.
Shortly before Christmas, other family members
fill the cluster unit with tales of the year's events.
I load the battery of my computer and my memory.
How far removed is that hotel in Zurich now.
A poem for you discovered in the front of her car.
For this reason, a poem about a Christmas tree,
a family gathering, an erstwhile love affair,
is nothing more than a *cadeau* for the reader who, like
La Rochefoucauld, knows: in every relationship
there is always one who does not receive a gift.

New Year

– translation by Charl JF Cilliers

At night in our house on the river,
that river which, every seven years,
rises to burst its unstable banks,
the ginger beer ferments in the pantry
beside fruity date-and-banana loaves.
A watermelon, sweet melon, peaches
are laid out for the New Year picnic
on the green banks of the sibilant Vaal.
A man catches a gigantic carp
and children squeal at a barbel slithering like a snake.
A ski-boat throws wild S-curves and beer bottles bounce
on the icy waters beside smouldering fires.
My mom in a floral dress and dad wearing a blazer,
always the perfect gentleman, listen to the cricket score
on a small radio. Everything was so swanky.
Uncle Johan, the health inspector,
complains about the municipality, and Aunty Six,
who now has Alzheimer's, whines about people of colour.
Be careful, warns mom. My sister
walks upriver with a man; I avoid
a young lieutenant's noxious stare. My eyes riveted
by a young girl rubbing on suntan lotion.
The polluted Vaal's flood surges are now long gone
and the Whites Only signs have come tumbling down.
And at night I hear the corks of ginger beer bottles popping in the
pantry of our-house-by-the river.

Christmas Time

– translation by Charl JF Cilliers

Children play cricket in the street,
the grown-ups sit around with a sundowner
talking about the first heart transplant:
Louis Washkansky with a young woman's heart.
My aunt holds a pale whisky, comments:
Surely not, a woman's heart in a man's chest?
Gran relishes a brandy and water, and my dear mom
nurses a gin and tonic, if my memory serves…
A bouncer breaks the window of the Voortrekker Hall:
we take to our heels when the factotum swears at us.
Next day my dad, the church elder, will fix what can be fixed.
From memories I've carried with me from way back then,
Denise Darvel's heart beat in his chest for 18 days.
Frank Sinatra sings that song most often sung:
Regrets, I've had a few, but then too few to mention,
Comme d'habitude.
There's more stone-throwing on the N2, my uncle grumbles.
On the stoep, they were complaining again about my nephew's hair
and his surfing. Above his bed in the outside room, Clint Eastwood
stokes the fires — *The Good, the Bad and the Ugly*:
for us it was LM Radio, jokes and sneaking a smoke.
Those long warm days in the Strand with a Christmas tree,
presents and, like my uncle's moustache, an expanse of lawn
in this perfect space, not a blade out of place, all absolute perfection.

The Drama of Being a Child
– translation by Charl JF Cilliers

What enchanted me most as a child
were the smells of summer fields.
The dam with its undisturbed water,
rushes in the vlei and tadpoles wriggling about,
frogs croaking, and even a snake under a stone,
glow-worms, grass seeds and fruit too poisonous to eat,
I remember as clearly as a dried-out bookmark
pressed skewly in *My Bible* at Isaiah.
Be careful of Bilharzia, my mother would warn us.
On top of the mountain, there was a half-built house
with a cement road and a *No Entry* sign.
That house was never completed; no one knows why.
Not then and not now either.
That house, the one that was never completed,
would later dog my footsteps. In Málaga,
I brushed against rough cement, took fright
at a piece of wire; the summer sun a seething yellow cobra.
And the dam with its putrescent water, also came looking
for me in a dream: entangled in those rushes,
I called for help, while water poured over the precipice.
How fragile and painful memory can be.
Smells, like tastes, are tangible, Neruda wrote somewhere.
A slice of pumpkin on my tongue still sings
of the taste of something wild, unsafe, tempestuously strange.

Travelling

– translation by Charl JF Cilliers

In search of my travelling companions,
a flight delayed —
no, in transit.
I unpack a suitcase for clean clothes,
worry something's been left on the plane.
The suitcase fans open,
refuses to take the dirty clothes;
the buckles break

become the rolling sounds
of a half-familiar song.

With my boarding pass ready
at the gate to resume the flight.
You are late.
As in all dreams,
I'm in a panic facing the locked gate,
until I see you, waiting for me,
my mother,

you, the salt of the earth,
you, the metre of my poems,

you, the one who encourages me to endure,
to never give up.

Solitaire

– translation by Johann de Lange

My family, compulsive bridge players,
could willingly
shuffle away a whole holiday
playing cards.
My father, especially, an excellent player,
could teach his scions
every trick of the trade.

But I was different.
From early on, I was immune to their clamour
or delight over a good hand

or a bluff,

as they sat together at a table
in a holiday town beside the sea.

Already, as a child,
I listened silently to the rhythm of the ocean
and placed imaginary bets
one after another on a roulette wheel.

My Dad

– translation by Johann de Lange

My dad
loved treating us
to a Sunday meal at the Masonic
or at uncle Boetie Michaels's hotel,
yes, the hotel still standing after the flood,
while his mother surveyed the scene from the deck of the Ark,
watching the off-sales being looted and the Vaal River bursting its banks.
I remember those Sunday menus:
tomato soup or bisque, fish and thinly carved leg of lamb
with overcooked vegetables. With ice cream or date pudding and custard…
And my dad smacking his lips sipping on a green Grünberger Stein…
I am writing this poem in an Italian restaurant
with an exotic poster of Venice on the wall.
Here you can put together your own menu:
Gnocchi or Cappelletti, perhaps Lamb Tortellini,
as if in a foreign country, a place with waterways
and gondolas and water taxis …
Not only did he introduce me to the delights of eating out,
my dad, no, he also imparted his belief that:
life is a menu,
one that you yourself compose,
with an unpayable bill.

Section III

Ars Poetica

Ring out the silences
I am nourished by.

– Allen Tate

In Emily Dickinson's Garden

– translation by Douglas Reid Skinner

Every day, Emily D believed
she heard the sounds of birds
in her tree-filled, lush, green garden.
It was here, in her garden of happiness,
as Judith Farr explained,
that she experienced the widest link
between poetry and gardening: from love to hate;
envy against virtue; death and eternity
dug into flowerbeds.
Planted wild fig marigolds, jasmines
and daisies. And picked a bouquet
each day for herself. And each flower
– even the gardenia –
looked up in flower encyclopaedias
– *Campanula*, Columbine, *Aquilegia* –
and therafter explored Webster's fields
as a traveller keeps track of her itinerary
in a strange country. Every
symbol precise, exactly understood.
O enigmatic woman in your white dress,
I visited your garden in the spring:
stood there and wondered
if you ever talk in the Garden of Eternity
with the other gardener of Amherst,
with her, Sylvia, whose death
keeps on blooming like a black arum lily?

Poetry, a Meditation

– translation by Charl JF Cilliers

Late at night in Chicago, I read of Paul Valéry
and how he grappled with great silences.
How does one articulate the greatest Abstraction?
For almost twenty years, it is said, he wrote
nothing after the death of his mentor, Mallarmé.
Silence and death, my mentor would caution me,
are the enemies of this poem; so blot it all out.
Late at night in Chicago, I read how Paul Valéry
struggled with his singular state of apoplexy.
The condition of Symbolism's great exponent
transformed into a clandestine, cantankerous still life.
Slowly the poem begins to swell from silence;
after all, igneous rock grows from so me stimulus.
In Louis Eksteen's *Afrikaans Synonym
Dictionary (with Antonyms)* a motto loudly proclaims:
All that lives must die,
passing through nature to eternity.
A pumpkin-yellow book from JL van Schaik,
unfortunately unobtainable now, published in 1981.
Before that great Silence smothers me,
I indulge in concrete images
– avoid abstract cries, listen to constructional contractions –
here late at night in Chicago, my kind of town,
delicately warding off and balancing the great Abstraction.

The Algebra of Pain
– translation by Charl JF Cilliers

for Johann de Lange

As we were walking down a farm road, could you ever have
imagined how life would ruthlessly strip away all illusions?
We both know the enslavement of this profession,
wrongly described as a quiet, lonely process.
On that farm road, stored away in the depths of memory,
a cold cellar of labelled bottles filled with sand,
you described the sickle moon as a broken finger nail.
So much discarded, endings, even murder in our lives.
Fata, you exclaimed. *Perhaps mere coincidence?*
For you, life, like death, a swift, grey phantom.
Tonight, far from that farm with a rusty
bucket in a poem and an owl calling out *hoo-hoo*,
I ask, purely as an act of mercy, that I, rather than you,
be the first to take leave of this inelegant poem – life.

Once More Lot's Wife
– translation by Charl JF Cilliers

A first memory
in a cemetery with lichens
and funeral flowers in broken glass holders.
The poem, even then, destined to be an *in memoriam*?
A second memory
of tiny houses and roads conjured out of buttons
and old corks on our winter carpet.
Already a sign of a flight from this bondage?
A third flashback,
more urgent, the dry course of a river bed,
caught up in something unmentionable
with the fragrance of poplar trees turning grey
and wintery dust wafting like admonition over everything:
too young for words, yet old enough for understanding.
Grieve for your youth, Alice Miller warned.
But how on earth can one do that?
Only a poem, a journey,
the uninterrupted movement,
the iterative-durative,
before the great standstill
can comfort me now
in this immutable condition
of utterly desolate distress.

The Unreliable Muse

– translation by Charl JF Cilliers

Our night in Luxor,
when you vanished
and I waited in the small cabin
listening to noisy passengers on the upper deck,
even the captain phoned: *is everything ok?*
Opening the porthole and seeing two lovers
in a neighbouring room
(two clumsy ships like tinned sardines side by side)
talking and loading photos of temples onto a screen,
which ones now I could not say,
perhaps Karnak? With a half-blind Nefertiti peeping out
on a postcard bought in a market,
with some bottled water,
Queen Hatshepsut in the Deir el-Bahri
enchanted you no end.
That night embodied all the elements
of the end of a relationship
and the beginning of a poem;
besides, I did not know then
that evidence was outpacing reality:
in the night, you vanished without a trace,
leaving me silent without an address
for that postcard,
a mere hieroglyph.
In a different kind of room,
I am still waiting for you:
a stanza, after all, is a place to pause, to wait.
Now morning light descends on the volta
of this damning poem.

Memorial Day: New York 25.5.2000

– translation by Johann de Lange

Commemorate the end of the war
because it rejuvenates poetry!
New York itself is a majestic poem
filled with contradictions like a destination on the West side
means something different than the same address on the East side;
that the poem will discard its dregs in Soho and the Bowery
defining it as superfluous, unnecessary, ugly;
added to this, that the subway is the unspoken unconscious,
like the way a poem addresses
the irreparable or perishable;
that somewhere, among these contradictory signs,
one finds a haven like Central Park,
the heart or kernel of the poem
(I will never, ever forget or forgive you); it begins
with a chance line like *A city decides*
the route for the traveller. The rhythm resembles
a jazz version of *Start spreading the news*,
implies the poet should know the original song.
Then follows the metre
and the awareness that a great poem resists scansion.
After all, it carries the whole world in the palm
of its hand. Against the NY skyline
with its tumbling twin towers…
A flood of impressions seizes the poet's mind.
Searching for a place to stay,
in the Hotel Prosody the poet bolts
her unconscious with a poem
brewed from sweat and blood.

Ariel

– translation by Johann de Lange

To write poetry you have to be prepared to die.

– Theodore Roethke

The brilliant girl
from Smith College
Phi Beta Kappa
(later on the editorial staff
of *Mademoiselle*)
screams silently,
her life balled up
underneath a bell jar.

The charming wife
of Ted Hughes
writes poems
at dawn before her baby's
first nursing
– becomes inexplicably nauseous,
cabbage burning
on the gas stove.

How bright the shards
of a broken jar shatter; how separate
the finger sliced open with a knife;
flowers blossom
like blood in the garden.

Dying
is an art, like everything else.
I do it exceptionally well.
Thus the intellect dissects
after yet another failed suicide attempt,
poplars are suicide trees...
copes with the daily household drill,
a wound-up metronome.

Death is an art
explored
in its finest details

– life, without question,
its copycat.

Section IV

Time and Eternity

Why has the music stopped?
Why is there such silence?

– Osip Mandelstam

Picasso – Guernica
– translation by Jo Nel

For select experts, an internal conflict
of childhood; fleeing with his parents
in earthquake-struck Malága, witnessing
deep in the night, the birth of his sister in a cave.
Those bolting horses, their hooves crashing,
haunt him, observes Alice Miller, psychoanalyst.

In the Museo Reina Sofia in Madrid, the guide relates
how at 16:30 on 26 April 1937 the Basque city,
as clear as yesterday, was bombarded for two hours
by Wolfram von Richthofen, apparently Hitler's
right-hand man and Francisco Franco's war contractor,
to thwart anarchists and socialists alike.

As for Pablo, the horses signify the people of Guernica;
for others, the bull or minotaur his primal power, logged
in my diary soon after our bullfight, a semblance

of just such an iterative-durative; external rebellion
resonates with internal carnage, just as
this poem – hoofless – onomatopoeically derails.

Beside Hieronymus Bosch's Triptychs
– translation by Douglas Reid Skinner

for Henning Snyman

I

Against my better judgement,
in the depths of the night, I summon up
those who have defiled my psyche
in the *Garden of Earthly Delights*.
But they cannot hear me;
their ears are pierced through
and a butcher's knife drives
them forward, away from my heart –
yes, that heart with a whistle
balanced on a de-
capitated head and
cloven body
in which strangers
make whoopee with my pain.
That this is hell, the self screams unprompted;
that this is hell, the self screams unprompted.

II

The lodgings with their emergency exit,
underfloor heating, Miró print,
a menu and tea and coffee caddy
for the traveller at the Auberge Burgundy,
sleepless, busy taking memories
from a suitcase and hanging them in the closet
without doors, next to an umbrella

probably left there in case
a storm outside should rage
in sync
with the storm inside.

III

Hyperbolic, you'd cry out.
No, I would counter. This poem
ignites a conflagration like the destructive fire
in 's-Hertogenbosch when the young
Jeroen Anthoniszoon van Aken observed
how flames disfigured the town of his birth.
A flying fish on which the young Jeroen
imagined riding in a later painting
shows how the destruction blossomed in his mind.
In *The Last Judgment*
the insane cannot hear
and a woman defies
the sexual overtures
of a snake.

IV

Years ago, I stood in the Prado
in front of the *Triptych of Epiphany*.
I know nothing of liturgy
or how the dead keep calling to us
long after they've departed. In my backpack,
a letter from Annette Theron
and her searing words
forever lodged in my mind.
In San Diego, I looked at the *Kiss of Judas*
suspended in time and space:
unaware-aware of what lay ahead…
Her final letter sent to me
on the day of her passing over.

V

Christ before Pilate hangs in São Paulo:
the *via dolorosa,* moving beyond words
in this poem, so clearly painted by Jeroen.
I, too, sing a beautiful song, a sad song
on my slender reed flute,
in this grammar of farewell
and holding onto you,
an expert on simplicity and ambiguity;
you who comprehends the miracles and destiny
of this disjunctive process:
non tarda, id est, strenuissima.

Poetry is a verdict, not an occupation
– translation by Douglas Reid Skinner

in memoriam Leonard Cohen (1934–2016)

The muddied affairs of my heart
syncopate with your dreamy, flowing songs.
At first black LPs that languidly
bid farewell to Marianne
and yearn for Suzanne;
then later grey tapes that crumple
and break, rewound too often,
to CDs with high fidelity versions
to which we dance until the end, the end…
Your waltzes became my waltzes
in the Tower of Song.
There was a flaw in everything,
but that's how the light
is able to break through,
become the cure, a device.
You are followed by many fans,
while my poem is just a calque
of timeless words.
Ring the bells that still can ring;
forget about perfecting the offering.
I salute you, Mr Cohen,
doff my fedora to you:
a singular poet-singer
of the melancholic word
with your exquisite, subsonic voice.

Lady Gaga

– translation by Douglas Reid Skinner

Do what you want
with my body, she taunts,
this imitation Marilyn.
Sometimes she sports a meat dress
that looks like Parma ham
hung in an authentic Italian restaurant.
She shows how raw she is inside,
this modern phenomenon.
Flesh bulges out, warns Lacan,
your character's expressed by the body.
Perhaps Marilyn crossbred with Madonna?
So authentic in her mimicking
of other icons, she even performs
Julie Andrews's songs from
The Sound of Music on an Oscar night.
What shall we do with this problem
called Lady Gaga?
Is she simply cracked, a crazy,
or a true emblem
that exaggeratedly
rides with bearing reins.
Let's not pluck out her tail feathers:
Lady Gaga the copycat
is unique and precious:
so, no salt on her feathers,
she's one for the gourmand.

Reeva

– translation by Douglas Reid Skinner

How could you know
on that last occasion
at the gates of the Silver House
and Red Bathroom,
a security officer
would play Saint Peter for you?
Was there a yellow aura glowing
around you, as Jung maintained,
when we knowing-unknowing and alone
make that crossing in complete solitude?
Could you have guessed that the fame
you sought would afford you pride of place
in the gallery beside JFK and Marilyn Monroe?
Your eyes closed just like Marilyn's
in the Brentwood morgue in Los Angeles;
your head blown open like Jack's.
How could you have thought that *Survivor* was only a prelude
to a court case with you as the present-absent?
Photos taken, even poached from the morgue,
are sold, montaged, pawned, mailed,
your eyes swollen as if in defence
against the absurdity, the distortion;
yes, even against this poem,
yet another public desecration.

Meditation, Time

– translation by Charl JF Cilliers

Time always connected with space: an SMS from you
on Brooklyn Bridge where the city waits for me.
I took a photo of the sturdy grey cables.
A bridge, contends Vladimir Propp in his study,
is a transition between two spaces: a coupling.
Our fairy tale is over, I know, in spite of your
efforts to reach out to me in another space and time.
Much later, I analysed *us* in my hotel on Times Square:
Absenteeism or departure from familiar surroundings (mine)
and a transgression of your request not to leave;
oh yes, I was the trickster who obtained information
about your double life and who, in your absence,
drew it out, point for point, like the cables of the bridge.
Propp talks of the difficult task or engagement,
the eventual reconciliation and the transfiguration.
Sadly, this poem shows too many of its cables and lanes.
On my return, with linear slowness, I studied
Morphology of the Folktale like a veritable philologist.
With the Brooklyn Bridge as a desktop background.

Adrienne Rich (1929–2012)

– translation by Charl JF Cilliers

What kind of beast would turn its life into words?

Few could, like you,
Ariadne,
hear a telephone ring in a dark labyrinth
in a time
when love between women
could unleash a war.
Your poems became an atlas
of this unsung exploration.
In a labyrinth with a thin, silver thread
to discover the concealed exit,
you steeled yourself against self-pity:
I love the scar-tissue she handed on to me,
but I want to go on from here with you
fighting the temptation to make a career of pain.
For the like-minded, you opened inner landscapes
exploring the length and breadth of intimate continents
in countless disturbing verses.
For you, poetry in actuality a *versus*.
You joined the battle-ready in opposing
injustice: senseless wars, censorship, oppression.
And my incurable anger, my unmendable wounds
break open further with tears, I am crying helplessly…
How does one square a labyrinth with an atlas?
In the still night, an imagined phone rings monotonously
with my window open: knowing you were right,
they are still the lawmakers, the cartographers
of love and this rhyming incarceration.
Her departure also imprisoned me in a dark labyrinth;
thanks to your intimate atlas I travelled to distant lands,

discovered imprudent delights
in remote expanses like Puerto Montt,
travelling past the equator
as far as Antarctica
where I planted a flag
in her oblivious heart.

To Dissect Sylvia Plath
– translation by Charl JF Cilliers

In the archaeological museum
of my tempestuous recollections,
I remember how, as a young child,
I read your 'Morning Song' out loud.
Saw how, exhausted, you listened
to the first sounds uttered by your child:
even then something intruded.
In my small white copy of *Ariel,*
written in capital letters:
Is she writing about Nicholas or Frieda?
Or perhaps about the birth
of a poem irrevocably demanding
a life outside of the poet?
I was barely sixteen then –
perhaps younger: my pencil strokes shimmer
soft up, hard down, soft up, hard down.
How hard of hearing all those around
you were: every letter to your mother
recounted your loneliness,
and what you locked up, wanted to avoid,
a second leave-taking, rejection, dismissal…
But you were coached for this kind of
thing: silently you dis-
engaged from him, your children,
for a last time posted a letter home.
The postman, alas, like a critic,
weighed it up, found it too heavy:
slapped on a sticker *Return to Sender,*
but there was no return address:
just the smell of gas through a tiny crack.

After a poem by Billy Collins ('Taking Off Emily Dickinson's Clothes')

Lucian Freud (1922–2011)

– translation by Charl JF Cilliers

Cantankerous Lucian
proved that where ego is, id will emerge.
Every painting lushly allowed these words
to flow out into strident portraits.
I am my art and my surroundings,
he growled to a critic, *and damn it, yes,*
I'll do as I see fit: after all,
the model won't be hanging beside the portrait!
Fleshy and fat was his grotesque Olympia.
I only do what I cannot relate.
So what was the obsession then, Mr Freud?
Perhaps the very thing your grandfather brooded over?
That fury is nothing more or less than melancholia?

When a Poet Dies

– translation by Charl JF Cilliers

tributes come streaming in
about the enormous loss and contribution
of our poet's voice, now silenced.

When a poet dies,
the literary undertakers stand waiting
with inflated assessments
of the squaring of his circle.

When a poet dies,
unseemly questions are asked
about his lifestyle, but seldom
whether he could write a rondel or a distich.

When a poet dies,
his work, if signed, is certainly
bought, then soon forgotten
till another poet takes his leave shortly after.

When a poet dies,
his poems just might inherit an enduring reader.

Todesfuge
– translation by Charl JF Cilliers

There is nothing on earth for which a poet would relinquish
his writing, not even if he were a Jew and the language of
his poems was German.
– Paul Celan

From a very young age,
you learnt the knack of
dancing with death. Your lectures
apparently sounded like prayers in a synagogue,
like muttered pleas for mercy, another chance...
On 20 April 1970, the Seine,
without map or vessel
would transport you wordlessly,
slowly and spasmodically
to a place far removed from the Shoah:
to rediscover there your broken parents.
Black milk of daybreak, we drink you in the morning.
Your hair was golden, hair now grown ashen...
Death is the master from Germany,
Death is the echo from France.
Ingeborg Bachmann's poems rise in song,
more meaningful and smouldering for haughty *colporteurs*.
Writing, a snake plagiarising and nestling on the breast.
Writing like lead drawing the poet down.
Black milk of daybreak, we drink you in the night.
You demand we perform a dance, a dance of death,
you whistle and a grave appears in the air.
O Margarete-Shulamith, have mercy on him,
this poet who could make and break language.
Black milk of daybreak, we drink and drink and avenge
ourselves in your bitter refrains:
your golden hair, Margarete,
your ashen hair, Shulamith.

Suicidaire
– translation by Joan Hambidge

To write poetry you have to be prepared to die.
– Theodore Roethke

Alvarez,
you had it wrong,
completely wrong
about this indecent thing called (suicide):
not only with rope or pills or poison or gas
or wrists spraying blood over the bath's rim.
Oh, I am the *suicidaire*,
the one who takes my life.
Alvarez,
you clench the cat by the tail
on this gruesome process called (suicide):
not only the note left behind,
pleading for forgiveness or understanding,
or a message left on a help line.
Oh, I am the *suicidaire*,
the one who takes my life.
Alvarez,
with every poem I take my life
in my hands as if it is (suicide).
With every verse where I turn back
to a personal Sodom and Gomorrah,
words are being weighed
like salt for that other kind of *suicidaire*.
Rather remember Vicente Huidobro.
Every superfluous adjective
in a poem commits murder,
a hackneyed image – a rope

strangling her in iambs,
uncrystallised confessions
are poisonous gases suffocating her.
Oh, I am the *suicidaire*,
the one who takes my life.

Programme Verse

– translation by Joan Hambidge

The swallows are departing:
the souls of the dead
leave silently
from south to north,
vertically and heavenward,
to an unknown, unchartered place,
a region where spiritualists say
the dead judge themselves;
where suicides and the murdered
slowly, if ever, find peace.
Clairvoyants can call them up;
highly developed mediums can sense their roaming
presences in old ransacked, spooky houses,
like trapped swallows in an airport terminal
flapping their wings in search of an exit,
blinded by windows frozen shut,
anxious because this unknown space
traps them and will not let go
on this obligatory journey without passport
or endorsed, special visa,
hand luggage or heavy, overloaded bag.
Sensitive youths can also see them:
lay an extra place at table
for the imaginary, visiting friend;
a savant from the elusive other side,
comforts a suffering person.
Mediums translate the messages yearned
for by a guilt-ridden family member.
And us? The ones left behind? The mourners?
The inheritors of mute, indecipherable postcards?
They leave us behind, confused, with the seed
we wished to feed, with the dried crumbs
of remorse, of I-still-wanted-to-say, to make amends:
banned from this mysterious winter journey.

Olga Kirsch (1924–1997)

– translation by Johann de Lange

Yiddish, it seems, has no word or concept
for disappointment, defeat, missed opportunity.
Nonetheless, in a foreign tongue,
you had to enter a second unapproachable exile.
A poet never betrays her heritage:
By the rivers of Babylon, there we sat down,
And, we wept, when we remembered Zion...
With your poems about the diaspora and persecution,
you named your people's grief.
How many words are there for pain?
Loneliness, illusion, sorrow, anguish, worry...
These you could capture, preserve and above all translate
into yearning, feverish songs.

Domanda
– translation by Joan Hambidge

for Margaret Rosabel Mezzabotta

Untimely, your premature exit
to an unknown region.
The soul, I remembered this morning,
is like wine that should mature slowly.
Becomes tainted
if hastily uncorked or poured.
You would immediately have been able to verify
this: recorded in the *Egyptian Book of the Dead*.
To comprehend your death
is an undecodable hieroglyphic
in an impassable, dark alleyway.
Death reverses the order of words,
it makes us look back, remember, even
seize small moments of chance –
like my cleaning your glasses once,
discussing dark symbols with you.
For this funeral oration, or reckoning
I am, as poet, completely unprepared —
no, rather, unwilling.
The so-called *consolatio* or comfort
of a medium (Look, she sends a rose)
or the flickering of a candle,
undoes nothing. What does 'passing away' mean? That you had to
leave – in my view anyway –
far too rapidly for heaven. That your soul
was forced out, seemingly without warning.
That roses fade,
candles cease to flicker...
Still I wanted to ask:
Who scratched out Nefertiti's one eye
so that she arrived blinded on the other side?

Poetry is a piece of very private history
which unobtrusively lets us
into the secrets of a man's life.

Henry David Thoreau

Poetry in its own way is ultimately mythology
the telling of the stories of the soul
in its adventures on this earth.

Stanley Kunitz

Afterword: Lost in Translation

This project has been brewing in my subconscious for many years. It commenced in 2000 after a visit to America to do research on a second doctorate on gender constructs. More recently, in 2016, the poem from *Indeks*, 'In Emily Dickinson's Garden' was translated for a paper presented at an international conference on comparative literature in Vienna. My paper was entitled 'Lost in translation' and dealt with the differences and similarities between my version of the translation and Douglas Reid Skinner's rendition.

It was a daunting task to make a personal selection of poems for this collection, as my volumes of poetry function as dioramas, with inter-textual references and various echoes between poems. Poems represented are from the original versions. I have always steered away from rewriting 'young' poems. On a few occasions I have made small renditions without tampering with the original autopsy report. 'Solitaire' is an example of a text that has been revisited and hopefully improved.

The selection is characterised by and focuses on main themes in my oeuvre – psychic underpinnings that recur throughout the collections: famous cities, love and family, *ars poetica*, and death and the passage of time. My first volume of poetry, *Hartskrif*, was written on the East Coast of America (New Haven) and many of my poems have been written on foreign shores; hence the many representations of cities in this anthology. An Afrikaans counterpart is *Die buigsaamheid van verdriet* (Protea, 2004), a selection of 100 poems from my oeuvre up to *Ruggespraak* (2002).

Gender issues are also addressed. The woman-identified-woman theme is obvious in my poetry. Emily Dickinson, Sylvia Plath and Anne Sexton are poetic icons.

Translating poems implies a post mortem, emotionally and poetically. Why does the poet, a coroner's wife, revisit certain themes and cities? What was the cause of death in a relationship? The image of the 'coroner's wife' implies the impossibility of the process – she is a mere onlooker.

Or as my poem 'Anne Sexton' (*Meditasies*, Human & Rousseau, 2014), states:

> You would write poetry about the coroner waiting on you,
> the devil, a fat Lazarus in a red suit. Mr. Mine.
> You were always cut in two. After your death,
> your poems and therapy sessions became the done thing.
> 'Riding the elevator in the sky,' beyond, beyond
> whirling, lingering gas with a key in your hand,
> 'that opens something –
> some useful door –
> somewhere –
> up there.'

Maybe Robert Frost was correct: what is *lost in translation* is the 'true' poem. Hopefully, in the 'carrying across' another is made.

Joan Hambidge
Cape Town, 2018.

Acknowledgements

I am indebted to Johann de Lange, poet and friend. And of course to Douglas Reid Skinner and to Jo Nel for their assistance and suggestions. Thanks to Charl JF Cilliers, who is the sole translator of *Lot se vrou* and *Meditasies*. I also followed advice from the poet Kim McClenaghan. A few poems were written in English and several translated by myself. Thanks are due to the editors of *Stanzas*, where some of these poems first appeared.

The Afrikaans versions of the poems translated in this collection first appeared in the following publications, in chronological order:

'In Emily Dickinson's Garden', 'Aubade' and 'Lady Gaga' in *Indeks* (Cape Town: Human & Rousseau, 2016)

'Name' and 'Reeva' in *Matriks* (Cape Town: Human & Rousseau, 2015)

'New York, a Meditation', 'Istanbul, a Meditation', 'Tokyo, a Meditation II', Los Angeles, a Meditation', 'Meditation, Family', 'Tokyo, a Meditation', 'Poetry, a Meditation', 'Meditation, Time', 'Adrienne Rich (1929–2012)' and 'To Dissect Sylvia Plath' in *Meditasies* (Cape Town: Human & Rousseau, 2014)

'Too Stony for Trees', 'My Dad', 'New Year', 'Christmas Time', 'The Drama of Being a Child', 'Dream', 'Travelling', 'The Algebra of Pain', 'The Unreliable Muse', 'Once More, Lot's Wife', 'Lucian Freud (1922–2011)', 'Todesfuge', 'Suicidaire' and 'When a Poet Dies' in *Lot se vrou* (Cape Town: Human & Rousseau, 2012)

'Tokyo', 'Kervansaray', 'Dublin', 'Santiago de Chile', 'Acapulco', 'Bangkok', 'Las Vegas, Nevada', 'Dallas, Texas' in *Visums by verstek* (Cape Town: Human & Rousseau, 2011)

'Photo: Man Falling', 'Ground Zero' and 'Memorial Day: New York 25.5.2000' in *Ruggespraak* (Pretoria: Protea Boekhuis, 2002)

'Programme Verse' and 'Domanda' in *Lykdigte* (Cape Town: Tafelberg, 2000)

'Solitaire' and 'My Dad' in *Ewebeeld* (Johannesburg: Perskor, 1997)

'State of Emergency' in *Donker labirint* (Cape Town: Tafelberg, 1989)

'Ariel' in *Die anatomie van melancholie* (Cape Town: Human & Rousseau, 1987)

'Rome' in *Hartskrif* (Cape Town: Human & Rousseau, 1985)

'Beside Hieronymus Bosch's Triptychs' and *'Poetry is a verdict, not an occupation'* are forthcoming in a new collection to be titled *Astrak*.

A final word of thanks to Michèle Betty for her work and support during this project.

Joan Hambidge

Notes on Epigraphs and Quotations

Phrases, epigraphs and quotations have been used, sometimes with and sometimes without acknowledgement from the following sources:

Page 9

Here, take this sand that I pour
From one palm to another

Osip Mandelstam, 'Not crediting the miracle of re-birth' in *The Selected Poems of Osip Mandelstam* (1891–1938) (New York: New York Review Books, 1973)

*

That was their business. As far as he was concerned.
Suffering was life's penalty; wisdom armed one
Against madness; speech was temporary; poetry was truth.

Robert Pinsky, 'Essay on Psychiatrists' in *Sadness and Happiness* (Princeton, New Jersey: Princeton University Press, 1975)

Page 13

He's forgotten utterly where he is.
He's forgotten Paddington, forgotten
Timetables, forgotten the long rocking
Cradle of a journey into the golden West...

Ted Hughes, 'Platform One' in *Ted Hughes: Collected Poems* (London: Faber & Faber, 2003)

Page 33

Love is a shadow.
How you lie and cry after it
Listen: these are its hooves: it has gone off, like a horse.

Sylvia Plath, 'Elm' in *Collected Poems* (New York: Harper Collins Publishers, 1992)

Page 35

Probatio pennae is the medieval term for breaking in a new pen and is used to refer to text or scribble written to test a newly cut pen.
Abent omnes uolucres nidos inceptos nisi ego et tu quid expectamus nu(nc) is roughly translated as, 'Have all birds except us begun nests – what are we waiting for?'

hebban olla vogala nestas hagunnan hinase hic enda thu wat unbidan we nu is the Old Dutch for the Latin sentence above.

Page 47

Ring out the silence
I am nourished by.

Allen Tate, 'Sonnets at Christmas' in *The Collected Poems 1919–1976* (New York: Farrar Straus & Giroux, 1932)

Pages 54 and 72

To write poetry: you have
to be prepared to die.

Theodore Roethke, in *On Poetry and Craft: Selected Prose of Theodore Roethke* (Washington: Copper Canyon Press, 1965)

Page 57

Why has the music stopped?
Why is there such silence?

Osip Mandelstam, 'Stone: 24' in *The Selected Poems of Osip Mandelstam* (1891–1938) (New York: New York Review Books, 1973)

Page 62

Poetry is a verdict, not an occupation

Leonard Cohen, *The Favourite Game* (Vintage, 1963)

Page 66

What kind of beast would turn its life into words? Adrienne Rich, 'Twenty-One Love Poems: Love Poem VII' in *The Dream of a Common Language Poems 1974-1977* (New York: W.W.Norton & Company, Inc, 1978)

Page 71

There is nothing on earth for which a poet would relinquish
his writing, not even if he were a Jew and the language of
his poems was German.

Paul Celan quoted by John Felstiner, in *Paul Celan: Poet, Survivor, Jew* (New Haven: Yale University Press, 1995)

Page 77

Poetry is a piece of very private history
which unobtrusively lets us
into the secrets of a man's life

Henry David Thoreau in *Henry David Thoreau – Ultimate Collection: 6 Books, 26 Essays &*
60+ Poems, Including Translations, Biographies & Letters (e-artnow, 2017)

*

Poetry in its own way is ultimately mythology
the telling of the stories of the soul
in its adventures on this earth.

Stanley Kunitz, 1994 Commencement Address at St Mary's College

Page 79

You would write poetry about the coroner waiting on you,
the devil, a fat Lazarus in a red suit. Mr. Mine.
You were always cut in two. After your death
your poems and therapy sessions became the done thing.
Riding the elevator in the sky, beyond, beyond
whirling, lingering gas with a key in your hand,
that opens something –
some useful door –
somewhere –
up there.

Joan Hambidge, 'Anne Sexton', a translation from the Afrikaans in *Meditasies*
(Cape Town: Human & Rousseau, 2014)

Translators' Biographies

CHARL JF CILLIERS has published nine volumes of poetry, the most recent being a collection of quatrains found in *Behind the View* (Malgas Publishers, 2014). His poems have appeared in various literary journals in South Africa and abroad including *New Coin, Standpunte, New Contrast, Ophir, Poet (India), Purple Renoster, De Arte, Chirimo (Rhodesia), Unisa English Studies, Seismograph, Out of the African Ark, Two Roads, 25/25, For All Seasons, Somewhere I Have Never Travelled* and *Life Is Poetry*. He was employed for over twenty years by Parliament as an editor and translator. In 1998, he retired as Editor of Hansard to the West Coast of South Africa where he devotes himself to writing.

JOHANN DE LANGE is the recipient of the Ingrid Jonker Prize 1983; the Rapport Prize for Poetry 1990; and the Hertzog Prize for Poetry 2011, as well as an Avanti award for his documentary script on the life of poet Ingrid Jonker. His poetry has been published in numerous collections, anthologies and journals. He has published twelve poetry collections, and two short story collections. He has translated Wilma Stockenström into English and Herman Charles Bosman into Afrikaans. He lives in Cape Town.

JO NEL read English and French for his BA, and went on to complete a PhD in modern English drama. He was a translator in the South African Air Force for six years before joining the University of the North as a faculty member in the Department of English. In 2003, he was seconded to Edupark, a non-profit company under the aegis of the University of Limpopo (the former University of the North). He retains his link to the University by remaining a faculty member. His interests are varied and he has read papers on Shakespeare in places like Los Angeles, Tokyo and Karachi, and papers on business education in Mauritius and the Seychelles. His interest in higher education management led to the provocatively entitled paper: 'The Academic as Whore or (S)laying Higher Education'. This paper was read at the IJAS conference in Las Vegas at the University of Nevada. Jo Nel is a member of the English Academy of Southern Africa and the SA Board for People Practices (Chartered HR Professional) and a board member of the International Business Conference (IBC).

DOUGLAS REID SKINNER has published seven collections, most recently *Liminal* (uHlanga, 2017). He has translated (on his own or with a co-translator) from Afrikaans, French, Hebrew, Italian and Portuguese. Publications of translation include: with Israel Ben-Yosef, *Approximations: Translations from Hebrew* (Carrefour Press, 1989); with Marco Fazzini, *The Secret Ambition: Selected Poems of Valerio Magrelli* (African Sun Press, 2016); and a selection of poems by Marco Fazzini translated from the Italian, *21 Poesie/Poemas/Poems* (Amos Edizioni, Italy, 2017). He is co-editor of *Stanzas* poetry magazine (Cape Town) and English editor and translator for the AVBOB Poetry Project.

WORKS IN THE DRYAD PRESS LIVING POETS SERIES

AVAILABLE NOW

An Unobtrusive Vice, Tony Ullyatt
A Private Audience, Beverly Rycroft
Metaphysical Balm, Michèle Betty

FORTHCOMING IN 2018

happier were the victims, Kambani Ramano
A Short History of Remembering, Stephen Symons

OTHER WORKS BY DRYAD PRESS (PTY) LTD

AVAILABLE NOW

Unearthed: A selection of the best poems of 2016,
edited by Joan Hambidge and Michèle Betty

Available from better bookstores in South Africa and online at
www.dryadpress.co.za or overseas at www.africanbookscollective.com

Printed in the United States
By Bookmasters